T0131743

Minnie the Hen Gets a Family

by

Wanda Perry

AuthorHouse™
1663 Liberty Drive
Bloomington, IN 47403
www.authorhouse.com
Phone: 833-262-8899

Because of the dynamic nature of the Internet, any web addresses or links contained in this book may have changed
since publication and may no longer be valid. The views expressed in this work are solely those of the author and do
not necessarily reflect the views of the publisher, and the publisher hereby disclaims any responsibility for them.

Any people depicted in stock imagery provided by Getty Images are models,
and such images are being used for illustrative purposes only.
Certain stock imagery © Getty Images.

This book is printed on acid-free paper.

ISBN: 978-1-4343-6480-7 (sc)
ISBN: 978-1-4817-3790-6 (e)

Print information available on the last page.

Published by AuthorHouse 10/08/2021

authorHOUSE®

Mr. and Mrs. Perené were an older couple who lived in a house over one hundred years old in a very old town. Their children had grown up and moved away from home, so they lived alone. Mr. and Mrs. Perené had no animals and did not plan to have any.

Then one day, a strange thing happened. When Mr. and Mrs. Perené returned home from a trip, there on the front lawn of their home, under a large tree, sat a cat and a hen. The cat and hen must have been friends, for they were sitting side by side and had apparently come together to this house. The Perenés had no idea why the cat and hen had shown up, but with the house being over one hundred years old, who knows? Maybe a long time ago the cat and hen had families living on a farm at this place and their instinct had guided them to return to the home of their grandparents, great-grandparents, or even great-great-grandparents.

Mr. and Mrs. Perené had no animals and were not prepared for animals; they assumed that the cat and hen would go home when night came. Mr. Perené, however, had quite a shock the next morning when he walked out into the backyard to find the cat and hen still there, actually looking as if they might want something to eat. It was quite clear to the Perenés then that the cat and hen had come to live with them and had somehow found themselves a place to sleep.

Well, Mr. and Mrs. Perené may not have had animals, but they knew that if a cat and hen mysteriously showed up and sat together under a big tree in their yard, they would certainly be fed and given names and a place to sleep. After much thought and consideration, the Perenés decided to name the hen Minnie. They named the cat Alley because she had dark gray fur with darker stripes and resembled an alley cat. Something about the appearance of Minnie and Alley gave the Perenés the idea that the two animals might have been a little on the wild side. They knew that since they had found their own sleeping places the night before, there was a good chance they were used to taking care of themselves and had their own ideas as to how they would live. "But," Mr. Perené asked Mrs. Perené, "Where were Minnie and Alley sleeping before they came to us?" "A cat and hen can't sleep on the ground and under bushes as the wild rabbits who come here do."

As it happened, it was not long before Allie decided to go live on a farm with friends of Mr. and Mrs. Perené. Minnie, however, did not wish to go live on the farm. She liked living in town with the Perenés, for she had found a place to roost in an outside storage shed which she preferred to the little henhouse that Mr. Perené had built in a safe place for her. The house Mr. Perené had built for her had lots of clean straw in it, but Minnie found an old bureau drawer in the Perenés' storage building and began using it as her nest. Soon Mr. Perené placed straw in the drawer, just in case Minnie should wish to lay eggs there.

Minnie seemed to be happy at the Perenés' home, and she stayed through different seasons. In the summertime, she would go about alone during the day, pecking in the garden and grass for insects or whatever she could find to eat. In the wintertime, when there was snow and not much to be found to eat in the garden, Minnie would eat at the bird feeders with the wild birds, but she would always go into the shed to roost at night. Minnie was a game hen, which is a type of chicken that is able to run fast and fly high, so if by any chance she was disturbed or scared while roosting, she would fly out the shed door and up to the top of a tall tree so she would be safe.

One day Mr. Perené said to Mrs. Perené, "You know, I haven't seen much of Minnie for several days; I'd better try to find her. He looked all around the large yard and even in the treetops, but he could not find her. He called for her as usual at feeding time, but she did not come. After a few days of this, Mr. Perené was desperate to find Minnie, so he decided to look in the storage building although it was day and he did not expect to find her there. Mr. Perené did not find Minnie on her roost, but she was on her nest in the drawer with her feathers all fluffed up around her. Now, Mr. Perené was not a farmer, but as he came closer to Minnie, she started clucking and squawking louder and louder and then pecking at him as he removed her from the nest. He knew that she had become a sitting hen and would not leave her nest because she wanted baby chicks. Mr. Perené knew she had laid eggs and that her motherly instinct was telling her to sit on the eggs day and night to keep them warm if baby chicks were to hatch from them.

It was just as Mr. Perené had suspected. When he finally removed Minnie from the nest, he found several eggs which she had been sitting on. Although Minnie had sat on the eggs for many days and had seldom left the nest, even for food and water, there was not one baby chick. Though Minnie was very protective and dedicated to sitting on the eggs, Mr. Perené knew that the eggs were not going to hatch and Minnie needed eggs from a farm to sit on.

When Mr. Perené had taken Minnie from the nest and away from the shed, she was so upset at being disturbed during her sitting that, clucking and squawking loudly, she flew over an old, tall wooden privacy fence and into a tall tree in the neighbors' backyard. Since Minnie was a little on the wild side and could fly into treetops to hide out and stay as long as she liked, Mr. Perené could not catch her; he could only sadly watch her go. Mr. Perené then went into the house and said to Mrs. Perené, "I think that Minnie may have gone to live with the neighbors," for he knew that Minnie could quickly make a home for herself just about anywhere.

What Mr. and Mrs. Perené did not know was that although Minnie enjoyed her home with them, she really wanted a family of her own, and she was very, very disappointed about having to leave her nest of eggs after having sat on them for days and days. Mr. and Mrs. Perené talked to each other about how they could help Minnie get a family if she should ever return to live with them. Finally, they came up with a plan.

In a few days, Minnie quit pouting and decided to come back to live with the Perenés. Now that they knew how serious she was about getting baby chicks, Mr. Perené placed more straw in the old drawer, and he and Mrs. Perené carried out the plan they had that would allow Minnie to have a family. They went to the country to visit a farm where the chickens and ducks had babies, and there they got eggs from their farmer friend for Minnie to sit on. The farmer told Mr. and Mrs. Perené that the eggs would have to be sat on for about twenty~one days if chickens were to hatch.

Sure enough, Minnie went back to her nest to start sitting again and was so excited and happy to find the eggs which had already been placed in her nest that she clucked and spread her wings over them as she once more began sitting on eggs and dreaming of getting a family. Minnie did not know how many days she would need to sit before the eggs hatched, but Mr. Perené remembered what the farmer had said about it taking twenty-one days for the eggs to hatch, so he placed food and water nearby for Minnie. As getting a family meant more than anything to her, she was happy to just sit on the eggs day after day and night after night.

One day Mr. Perené went to give food and water to Minnie and he heard a peep. Moving closer, he looked into the nest and saw one baby chicken next to Minnie and another one peeping out from beneath her. Minnie scolded Mr. Perené and clucked loudly. She did not want him coming close to her nest, and she actually wanted the baby chicks to stay beneath her wings without even peeping out. As the hours went by, however, the chicks grew stronger and it was hard for Minnie to keep them under her wings or even in the nest.

After another day or two, when Mr. Perené came back, there were four baby chicks, or biddies, in the nest with Minnie.

Soon Minnie's babies grew a little bigger and stronger, and she felt that if she could stay close to them, they could go about the yard so they could get some sunshine and she could teach them how to hunt for food. When Minnie took her family out into the yard, Mr. Perené saw that she had not four, but five baby chicks.

The Perenés felt they should share this excitement and happiness with someone, so they set a time for the children who lived along their street to come and see Minnie and her family. Most of the children had not seen a hen with her baby chicks before, and they were very excited, not only about the little chickens, but also about the way their mother protected them. Mr. and Mrs. Perené were overjoyed because they finally knew that Minnie not only had a good home, but also the family she had worked and waited for so long.

Printed in the United States
by Baker & Taylor Publisher Services